T3-BHD-920

ROD

LEATHERBACK TURTLES, GIANT SQUIDS,

AND OTHER MYSTERIOUS ANIMALS OF THE

DEEPEST SEAS

EXTREME ANIMALS IN EXTREME ENVIRONMENTS

ANA MARÍA RODRÍGUEZ

E **Enslow Publishers, Inc.**
40 Industrial Road
Box 398
Berkeley Heights, NJ 07922
USA

http://www.enslow.com

For my husband and sons, who share my journeys through extreme worlds

Acknowledgments

The author expresses her immense gratitude to the scientists who so kindly gave their time to comment on the manuscript and provided images to illustrate the book. Your help has been extremely invaluable.

Library of Congress Cataloging-in-Publication Data

Rodriguez, Ana Maria, 1958–
  Leatherback turtles, giant squids, and other mysterious animals of the deepest seas / Ana María Rodríguez.
    p. cm. — (Extreme animals in extreme environments)
  Includes bibliographical references and index.
  Summary: "Explains why the ocean depths are extreme environments and examines how leatherback turtles, giant squids, and other animals have adapted to the harsh conditions"—Provided by publisher.
  ISBN 978-0-7660-3696-3
  1. Deep-sea animals—Juvenile literature. 2. Marine animals—Juvenile literature. 3. Ocean
—Juvenile literature. I. Title.
  QL125.5.R63 2012
  591.779—dc22

                              2010037576

Paperback ISBN 978-1-4644-0019-3

ePUB ISBN 978-1-4645-0466-2

PDF ISBN 978-1-4646-0466-9

Printed in the United States of America

092011 Lake Book Manufacturing, Inc., Melrose Park, IL

10 9 8 7 6 5 4 3 2 1

To Our Readers: We have done our best to make sure all Internet addresses in this book were active and appropriate when we went to press. However, the author and publisher have no control over and assume no liability for the material available on those Internet sites or on other Web sites they may link to. Any comments or suggestions can be sent by e-mail to comments@enslow.com or to the address on the back cover.

♻Enslow Publishers, Inc., is committed to printing our books on recycled paper. The paper in every book contains 10% to 30% post-consumer waste (PCW). The cover board on the outside of each book contains 100% PCW. Our goal is to do our part to help young people and the environment too!

Illustration Credits: Anna Fiolek / NOAA Central Library, p. 13; Bruce Mora, p. 16; Charleston Bump Expedition 2003 / NOAA Office of Ocean Exploration / Dr. George Sedberry, South Carolina DNR, Principal Investigator, p. 14; Enslow Publishers, Inc., p. 6; Estuary to Abyss 2004 / NOAA Office of Ocean Exploration, p. 33; Image courtesy of NOAA / NIWA, p. 40; Image courtesy of NOAA-OE, p. 41; © 2004 MBARI, p. 30; Museum of New Zealand Te Papa Tongarewa, MA 1.089076, p. 35; National Aeronautics and Space Administration (NASA), p. 9; NOAA / Monterey Bay Aquarium Research Institute, p. 22; NOAA Archive / Courtesy of Edie Widder, p. 28; NOAA Photo Library, p. 19; © Oceanlab, University of Aberdeen, UK, pp. 31, 32; Operation Deep Scope 2005 Expedition / NOAA Office of Ocean Exploration, p. 34; Pacific Ring of Fire 2004 Expedition / NOAA Office of Ocean Exploration / Dr. Bob Embley, NOAA PMEL, Chief Scientist, pp. 38, 39; Photograph by Dudley Foster from RISE expedition, courtesy of William R. Normark, USGS, p. 37; © 2011 Photos.com, a division of Getty Images. All rights reserved, pp. 3, 21; © Rowan Byrne / SeaPics.com, pp. 24, 25; Shutterstock.com, pp. 1, 4.

Cover Illustration: Shutterstock.com (Leatherback turtle).

CONTENTS

1 THE MYSTERIOUS DEEP BLUE OCEAN

This is a yellow anglerfish. There are more than two hundred species of anglerfish, most of which live in the darkest depths of the Atlantic and Antarctic oceans.

In 1869, Jules Verne wrote his book *Twenty Thousand Leagues Under the Sea*. Sixty-one years later, the fictional deep-sea explorations Verne created came true. In 1930, William Beebe and Otis Barton descended for the first time in a steel, sphere-shaped submersible called the bathysphere to a record-breaking depth of 1,584 feet (435 meters).[2] They had attached a dead fish to the outer surface of the bathysphere to attract creatures of the deep sea, and this worked well. Through the 3-inch- (8-centimeter) thick quartz windows, they were the first to observe amazing deep-sea creatures in their natural habitat. For Beebe, this was "a world as strange as that of Mars."[3]

In subsequent dives, Beebe and Barton descended to a maximum of 3,000 feet (914 meters). Using a telephone line connecting the bathysphere to the ship on the surface, Beebe radio broadcast his experiences:

1,500 feet (457 meters): "Black as Hades." (In Greek mythology, *Hades* is the underworld kingdom inhabited by the souls of the dead.)

1,550 feet (472 meters): "There is plenty of light down here now."

Gloria Hollister, an assistant aboard the surface ship, asked Beebe through the phone: "Can you give the light a color?"

A map of the planet's oceans: Pacific, Atlantic, Indian, Southern, and Arctic.

Dr. Beebe shouted: "It varies from pale blue to pale green. But all on the very pale side. No deep tone. It must be the normal luminescence of the creatures. . . . Gosh, it's cold"[4]

"Wear your flannels next time," Miss Hollister said.[5]

The ocean is the least studied habitat on the planet. Every time a deep-sea expedition returns, it brings back species that are new to science. One of the reasons is that, for the most part, the ocean is one of the most extreme environments on Earth.

OCEANS OF THE WORLD[6]		
OCEAN	Surface Area (million mile² / million km²)	Average Depth (feet / meters)
Pacific	59 / 153	13,957 / 4,254
Atlantic	32 / 83	12,100 / 3,688
Indian	26 / 68	12,762 / 3,890
Southern	7.7 / 20	10,627 / 3,239
Arctic	3.5 / 9	8,189 / 2,496

Which is the largest ocean? Which is the second largest? Which is the deepest (in average)? Which is the second deepest?

THE BLUE IN THE BLUE PLANET

Seen from space, Earth's predominant color is blue because about 70 percent of its surface is underwater. The ocean is the largest habitat of the planet. About 85 percent of the ocean is more than 5,280 feet (1,609 meters) deep. At this depth and below, the ocean is totally dark, almost freezing cold, and applying pressure high enough to crush a golf ball.[7] The ocean holds about 98 percent of the total volume of water on the planet. The other 2 percent is freshwater (rivers and lakes), groundwater (underground), atmosphere water, and frozen water trapped in glaciers and ice caps.

CONSTANT MOTION

The ocean is in constant motion. Winds power waves, the pull of the moon determines the tides, and differences in water temperature and salt content at different depths drive the underwater currents. These currents circulate constantly around the planet, mixing cold and warm waters, which affect local climates.

However, the temperature of the surface water varies a great deal around the planet. On the equator, temperatures are very warm, sometimes about 88° Fahrenheit (31° Celsius). In the polar regions, surface waters are extremely cold (28°F or −2°C).[8]

Also, the deeper it is, the colder the water will be, reaching closely to the seawater freezing temperature of 28.6°F (−1.9°C). Seawater freezes at a lower temperature than freshwater (32°F or 0°C) because it is salty.

SALT AND GAS OF THE OCEAN

The ocean's salinity—or the amount of minerals it contains—is about 35 grams per liter of seawater. The majority of the minerals

Our blue planet as seen from space by *Apollo 17* in 1972.

WHERE DOES THE WATER IN THE OCEAN COME FROM?

Scientists have not agreed on an answer to this question yet. Some say that the oceans formed by condensation of the enormous clouds of water vapor present in the atmosphere as Earth cooled down. Rain fell in huge amounts and filled up the basins, or sinks, of the planet.

Another idea is that the water came from outer space. Asteroids and comets have pelted Earth since its early beginnings. Asteroids are big chunks of rock that contain a lot of water. Comets—called "dirty snowballs"—are mountain-sized blocks of frozen water mixed with rocks. The oceans may have formed as these enormous space bodies struck Earth and released the water inside.

Maybe the oceans formed by a combination of terrestrial and extraterrestrial events.[9]

are sodium and chloride—the components of table salt.

The ocean also has dissolved gases. Oxygen is one of the most important gases because living organisms need oxygen to survive. The colder the water is, the more oxygen it carries.[10] Carbon dioxide, the gas living creatures breath out, is important for plantlike algae. They use it to produce nutrients through the process of photosynthesis.

LIGHT, SOUND, AND THE OCEAN

Water interacts with light. When light waves travel from air to water, they slow down and light bends, or is refracted. Particles suspended in water scatter light. Heat is absorbed by water, warming it up. All colors of the spectrum, except blue and green, are quickly absorbed by water. Water reflects blue and green, and that is why the ocean looks mostly blue.

But even blue and green can go only so deep. These colors are completely absorbed at about 3,280 feet (1,000 meters) deep, making the ocean totally dark.

Water interacts with sound.[11] Sound travels through water about four times faster than through air. The speed of sound depends on the temperature, the salinity, and the pressure of the water. At 3,280 feet (1,000 meters) below the surface, these factors combine to produce a zone called SOFAR (SOund Fixing And Ranging). Sounds produced in SOFAR, like a whale trying to locate a mate, for example, travel horizontally only, rather than in other directions. These sounds reach across entire oceans. Because seawater transmits sound better than light, hearing in water is a very important adaptation for many marine creatures.

EXTREME GEOGRAPHY UNDER THE SEA

There are mountain ranges, valleys, and trenches under the sea, just as there are on land. And more than one-third of the ocean floor is flatter than the state of Kansas.[12] The tallest mountain on Earth measured from the base to the peak is not Mount Everest but a dormant underwater volcano in Hawaii called Mauna Kea (33,476 feet or 10,203 meters). The deepest trench under the ocean is the Mariana Trench, which is 35,840 feet (10,924 meters) deep. It is located in the North Pacific Ocean, east of the Philippines.

UNDER THE SEA

The ocean is an enormous habitat that offers a variety of conditions for animals to live in. Scientists have divided the ocean column into five major zones according to depth.

THE OCEAN ZONES					
Zone	Range (feet / meters)	Solar Radiation	Temperature (F/C)	Pressure (atmospheres)*	Food Supply
Epipelagic or photic	Surface to 656 / 200	Abundant, seasonal	38.8–40.8 / 3.8–4.9	1 to 20	Abundant: seasonal, primary producers (photosynthesis), consumers, and decomposers
Mesopelagic or twilight	656 / 200 to 3,280 / 1,000	Twilight (green-blue)	Drops quickly with depth	20 to 100	Limited: consumers, sea snow, decomposers
Bathypelagic	3,280 / 1,000 to 13,120 / 4,000	None	28.6 / −1.9	100 to 400	Very limited: sea snow, consumers, decomposers

* one atmosphere is the pressure felt at sea level

The Abyssopelagic and Hadalpelagic zones are like extensions of the Bathypelagic zone down to the bottom of the ocean that support even sparser fauna. The sea floor is the benthic zone, with no precise depth.

2
LIVING BENEATH THE SEA

The animals of the sea are called plankton, nekton, and benthos.

PLANKTON: DRIFTING IN THE OCEAN

Plankton refers to organisms that cannot resist the power of the currents. Some swim, but not powerfully enough to avoid drifting, such as jellyfish or jellies. Other animals do not swim. Plankton has been found at all depths.

There are two kinds of plankton: the phytoplankton and the zooplankton. Phytoplankton organisms are like the

Jellies may be large or small and live in warm or very cold waters.

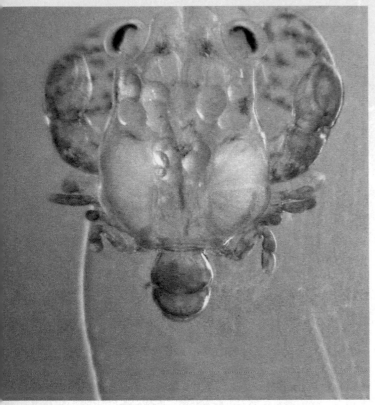

A crab larva is an example of zooplankton.

plants of the sea but so tiny they are only visible through a microscope. They are the primary producers of the ocean. They produce all the food consumers eat using carbon dioxide, water, and light to power photosynthesis. Zooplankton feeds on the phytoplankton. Krill are an example of zooplankton that in turn feed larger animals, such as fish and whales.

NEKTON: THE POWERFUL SWIMMERS

Nekton refers to animals that swim powerfully enough to overcome currents. Think of fish, such as tuna and sharks, and of marine mammals, like dolphins and whales. Nekton organisms, such as dolphins and whales, are mostly epipelagic because they need to breathe air. Other organisms, such as tuna and leatherback turtles, feed in the epipelagic zone and dive deep on occasion looking for food or avoiding predators.

BENTHOS: LIFE AT THE BOTTOM OF THE SEA

Benthos includes the animals living on the seafloor, such as clams, crabs, and blobby sea cucumbers. Some of them, such as corals, attach themselves to rocks or another solid surface on the bottom. Others—think sea cucumbers, crabs, and sea stars—crawl on top of the seafloor.

Life across the ocean is a major challenge. Marine creatures have to keep up in the water, find and catch food, and deal with low temperatures. On top of this they have to avoid hungry predators, find a mate, and have their young. How do they do it?

KEEPING UP IN THE WATER

Birds have to flap their wings or glide to counter gravity and stay up in the air. In a similar way, marine animals need to counter gravity to avoid sinking. One of their strategies is using floating devices.

Most plankton do not sink because their bodies are full of oil or wax droplets. Oil and wax are less dense than water, so they float. Larger drifters, such as the Portuguese man-of-wars, have a floating device filled with gas. It looks like an inflated clear plastic bag. The meters-long stinging tentacles of the man-of-war hang beneath the floater.[1]

This tiny and very dangerous Portuguese man-of-war measures only an inch across.

Nekton, such as fish like tuna and sharks, and mammals, such as dolphins, whales, and seals, swim fast to stay at the depth they want to be. They swim at the surface chasing a school of fish or deeper below avoiding a predator or socializing with others of their kind. Swimming demands a lot of energy, so these animals have to eat enough food to keep up with their lifestyle.

Other fish have an internal air-filled pouch—the swim bladder—that works like a floating device. Tuna and sharks do not have a swim bladder, but many bony fish like the mackerel do.[2] The nautilus is a soft-bodied creature with tentacles. It lives inside a coiled

WHY DO BODIES SINK?

A body sinks when its density (mass divided by volume) is greater than the density of the water around it. Bone and muscles (protein) that make up a fish, for example, are denser than seawater. On the other hand, oils, fats, gelatin, and gases are less dense than water. When a marine creature has dense bones and more muscle than oils, fat, gas, gelatin, or even water inside the body, it will sink. When an animal has more oils, fats, air, gelatin, or water inside its body than muscle or dense bones, then it will be buoyant or float.

shell with air-filled chambers, which help it float. Cuttlefish have many small air-filled chambers in their hard cuttlebone.

Dolphins, whales, and other marine mammals have lungs. The air in their lungs helps them float. However, when marine mammals dive below certain depths, the pressure collapses their lungs, eliminating their "floating device," and they sink. Interestingly, marine mammals have learned to take advantage of this problem. They sink effortlessly until they reach the desired depth, saving energy. They use the energy saved to stay longer underwater finding prey or avoiding predators.[3]

Deeper in the water column there are fish that neither swim fast, nor have a swim bladder. They keep up in the water because their bones are less dense, and they have less muscle mass and more fat in their bodies. Deepwater sharks have very large livers that take 65 percent of their body cavity and are filled with fats. Shark's skeletons are made of cartilage, which is less dense than bone.[4] The bodies of jellyfish-like creatures are over 80 percent water, which reduces their overall density.

FINDING FOOD

Sight is a very important sense in the epipelagic zone, where light is abundant and there is no place to hide from predators. Fish, small squids, and marine mammals that frequent this zone have good eyesight and typically large eyes.

Fish also have a remote sensing system called the lateral line, which detects vibrations in the water. They use this to detect predators and to stay in touch with schoolmates. Most fish like tuna and sharks have very good hearing. They are strongly attracted to splashes in the water, the kind of vibration injured fish make. Sharks have a very important sense called the electrical sense. They are capable of sensing other organisms' electrical fields and use the fields to track them.

Because predators rely so much on vision to find prey, the prey use vision to get away (camouflage). One way to become almost invisible to predators is to be transparent. Tiny zooplankton called amphipods, jellies, and salps are very hard to see in the water. Other animals use "countershading." Their backs are green, blue, or black, and their bellies are white or silver. When a predator looks down, the deep ocean looks dark blue. So, seen from above, a fish with a dark back will blend in with the dark background of the deep sea. If a predator looks up toward the surface, it sees bright light. A fish with a white or silver belly will blend well with the bright background, and it won't be easy for a predator to see it.

Many animals have learned to use sound in various ways. Whales and dolphins produce sound to communicate with each other over long distances. Dolphins and whales also use sound, called echolocation, to locate prey and predators.

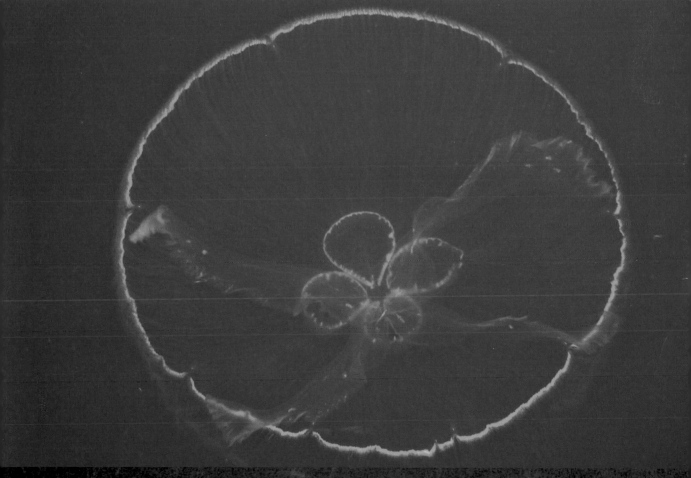

This jelly has adapted to living in areas where background light is in a constant state of flux. Transparency hides the animal from potential predators.

In the twilight zone where the light is dim, many animals have large, light-sensitive eyes, which can see even with little light. At this depth, vision is still important for preying and avoiding predators. Many animals use countershading and are transparent, especially in the upper levels where there is some light. Deeper in this zone, fish tend to be more silver. In the deepest zones, zooplankton are often red, orange, or purple.[5] Red is a good color to use as camouflage deep in the twilight zone because it appears dark in a dark background, making the animal practically invisible.

Many sea creatures have chemoreceptors, or taste sensors, which detect chemicals in the water. People have them on the tongue, but octopuses have them on their suckers, and some fish have them along their bodies.

CATCHING FOOD

The number one rule of survival for any living organism is to find enough food. Marine animals use a variety of strategies. Most animals catch their food with their mouths.

Some animals are filter feeders. They swim to the epipelagic zone, swallow seawater, and filter huge amounts of tiny plankton. Baleen whales, such as the blue and the gray whale, have hundreds of vertical plates (baleen) attached to the upper jaw. The plates are flexible and have hairlike projections that filter small prey, such as krill, that the whales swallow. Fish and other mammals have jaws lined with teeth.

An octopus may live close to the surface in warm waters, as well as in deep, cold waters.

Turtles do not have teeth but have hard, sharp plates that trap and cut prey. Octopus, squid, and cuttlefish use their long arms and tentacles with suction cups and hooks. Squids have a sharp beak they use to cut prey. Jellies capture prey with their long, poisonous tentacles.

Many animals move about to find prey. Fish and mammals, such as whales, swim by propelling their bodies with their tail fins. Sea snakes move in a similar way as land snakes do. Reptiles, such as turtles, marine iguanas, and crocodiles, spend their lives both in water and

Deep-sea mushroom coral attach to solid surfaces and feed on what currents bring to them.

on land. They use their limbs as paddles to move about the water. Octopus, squid, and cuttlefish propel themselves by squirting water from their bodies. The mysterious and wonderful dumbo octopus uses flapping earlike "wingfins" to swim!

Benthos organisms, such as sponges, corals, and anemones, which live on the sea bottom, do not move at all. They attach their body to a solid surface and catch prey that comes to them. Sponges are filter feeders, while corals and anemones capture prey using tentacles and poisonous stingers. Sea cucumbers, which are relatives of sea stars, crawl on the bottom, sucking up other creatures' remains.

ENDOTHERMS: MAKING THEIR OWN HEAT

The deeper animals dive, the colder the water becomes. Sea animals have a variety of strategies to keep up with the cold.

Mammals and birds are endotherms, or warm-blooded. Their body temperature is practically constant regardless of the outside temperature, because it depends on the heat produced inside their bodies by their metabolism.

Marine endotherms, such as sea lions, whales, and dolphins, produce body heat constantly but also minimize heat loss with a thick layer of blubber, or fat, under their skin. Fat insulates their bodies, or reduces the passage of heat, keeping them warm longer. Polar bears, which are considered marine mammals because they spend most of their time on sea ice, complement their blubber with thick fur. Penguins also have fat under their skin, which they insulate even more with a dense coat of feathers. Feathers and hair keep animals warm because they trap warm air.

Endotherms also reduce the amount of blood that circulates on the surface of their fins to limit heat loss. Sometimes, they use a "countercurrent" system. In dolphins, for example, the main artery carrying warm blood is located deep within the flipper. It is surrounded by veins carrying colder blood returning to the body core, which

THE LEATHERBACK TURTLE

The leatherback turtle is the largest turtle. It can be as long as a man is tall (5.9 feet long or 1.8 meters), but much heavier (almost 1,102 pounds or 500 kilograms). It is also very well adapted to the marine environment. Its carapace (the only soft shell among turtles) has ridges that make swimming easier. The front flippers are very powerful and longer than those of other sea turtles. These characteristics help leatherback turtles take on extremely long migrations along the oceans. They take long journeys to find their birthplace and lay their eggs on warm beaches. They also swim long distances looking for cold waters with abundant food.

Turtles are reptiles (ectotherms), but leatherbacks can be very active even in the cold waters of the North Atlantic. They are in between cold- and warm-blooded animals, such as tunas and sharks.[6] They have several adaptations that allow them to maintain a body temperature that is warmer than the surrounding water. For example, leatherbacks have a large body size, which cools down slower than a smaller body. They reduce heat loss by having a countercurrent blood flow (tunas and sharks share this strategy) and a thick layer of fat. Leatherback turtles eat immense amounts of jellies. They catch them by diving deeper than any other turtle—to extreme depths of 3,937 feet (1,200 meters) for 85 minutes.

Baby leatherbacks are so small that children can hold them in their hands

Adult leatherback
turtles can carry a
child on their backs.

then warms up as it passes beside the warmer artery. Despite all the mechanisms to reduce heat loss, endotherms must eat frequently to maintain their metabolism.

ECTOTHERMS: COLD BODIES

All animals other than birds and mammals are ectotherms, or cold-blooded animals. The body temperature of amphibians, octopuses, squids, starfish, and most fish and reptiles, for example, is determined by the environment. Some ectotherms move to the epipelagic zone when they need to warm up their bodies. They move down to cooler zones to cool down. Their bodies work at a slower pace than endotherms. For this reason they need less food than endotherms on a daily basis.

The Antarctic ice fish and the winter flounder live in water as cold as the freezing point of seawater (28.6°F or −1.9°C). But these fish do not freeze. They have antifreeze molecules in their blood that prevent the formation of deadly ice crystals inside their bodies.[7]

3
LIVING IN THE MOST EXTREME ENVIRONMENTS

The deepest ocean zones challenge animal survival in unique ways. When light and warmth totally disappear; when pressure can crush most bodies; and when food is extremely rare, how do deep-sea animals cope?

BIOLUMINESCENCE: THE LIVING LIGHT

In the absence of light, some animals make their own. Many animals from the mesopelagic zone have photophores, or light-producing organs, along their bodies in patterns that vary with the type of creature. The glow is usually green-blue and matches the color and brightness of the light coming from above. This is a form of camouflage called counter-illumination. Some predators have eyes that can detect the subtle differences between bioluminescence and natural light. Bioluminescence is produced by special bacteria that live within the bioluminescent animal or by the animal itself.

Note the green fluorescence of the eyes of this short-nose, green-eyed fish.

Jellies are bioluminescent all over their bodies. Some shrimps squirt out bioluminescent fluids, and some octopus and squid produce bioluminescent ink. Bioluminescent secretions probably work as a defense mechanism, as is the case of the green bombers. Some animals, such as the anglerfish, use bioluminescence to lure prey. Dragonfish, on the other hand, who can see red while most other animals cannot, have red-colored headlights that allow them to see in their totally dark environment.

In the deepest sea zones, animals do not need to worry much about color because there is no sunlight. Interestingly, bioluminescence is not very common in the deepest parts of the ocean for reasons that are not clear yet. In the deepest zones, animals have very small eyes, or they are blind.[1]

DEALING WITH PRESSURE: WHY THE PRESSURE DOES NOT CRUSH DEEP-SEA ANIMALS?

The deeper marine creatures dive, the higher the pressure they feel on their bodies. The water does not crush them because their bodies apply the same pressure toward the water as the water applies to them. Most do not have air chambers the pressure would crush.

THE GREEN BOMBERS

There is no better name for this worm than *Swima bombiviridis*. This tongue twister of a name means that this worm can swim and carries green "bombs" that look like tiny glowing water balloons. The worms swim in the deep, dark ocean in a snake-like manner and are half as long as a pencil and about the same thickness. They propel their bodies with numerous bristles that form a line of paddlelike structures along each side of their bodies.

Scientists were fascinated when they discovered that the worms have a curious defense strategy. They drop balloonlike pouches—scientists call them "bombs"—from their bodies when they feel threatened. The bombs glow green for several seconds. Scientists think that the bombs distract predators, allowing the worm to escape. The worms live in a pitch-black environment, so the sudden appearance of green light floating around will catch the predator's attention for a few seconds. This is long enough for the worm to wiggle away into the darkness.[2]

The barreleye (*Macropinna microstoma*) has tubular eyes capped by bright green lenses. The eyes point upward (as shown here) when the fish is looking for food overhead. They point forward when the fish is feeding. The two spots above the fish's mouth are olfactory organs called nares, which are similar to human nostrils.

THE AMAZING BARRELEYE FISH

Using its large, flat fins, the barreleye fish floats practically motionless in the dark about 2,297 feet (700 meters) under the sea near Monterey Bay, California. Nevertheless, the barreleye fish has no trouble finding food. It has tube-shaped eyes inside a transparent head. The eyes capture the dimmest outlines of prey above its head, focusing with bright green lenses. But the eyes are not aligned with the mouth. How does this fish capture its prey? Bruce Robison and Kim Reisenbichler at the Monterey Bay Aquarium Research Institute (MBARI) observed a barreleye fish by using high-resolution color video cameras mounted on a remotely operated vehicle (ROV). As the scientists guided the ROV around a barreleye fish floating deep in the ocean, they observed that the fish's eyes rotated inside its head. They moved from looking upward to looking forward, aligned with the mouth and back. What an intriguing way to "keep an eye" on their prey![3]

Only if they swim to a different zone will they be affected by the differences in pressure.

NO FOOD

Just about 5 percent of the food produced in the epipelagic zone makes it to the deep sea. The food comes down as sea snow. Sea snow contains the remains of animals, phytoplankton, and microbes

The deep sea is not a deserted place. Here is a sample of what thrives more than 4.3 miles deep in the Peru-Chile Trench.

A new species of snailfish was found 4.3 miles deep in the Peru-Chile Trench in 2010.

SCIENCE IN PROGRESS: HOW DEEP DO OCEAN CREATURES LIVE?

Sea cucumbers—blobby, sausage-shaped relatives of the starfish—have been found in the Mariana Trench, the deepest in the world. The snailfish is the deepest-known fish, for now. Scientists from Aberdeen (Scotland), Tokyo, and New Zealand filmed it swimming in the Japan Trench 4.8 miles (7,700 meters) deep in 2008.[4] The pressure at this depth feels like 1,600 elephants standing on the roof of a small car.[5] The same scientists found a new species of snailfish and a group of very active eels at 4.3 miles (7,000 meters) deep in the Peru-Chile Trench in 2010.[6] What will scientists discover next?

A group of eels actively feed 3.7 miles deep in the Peru-Chile Trench in 2010.

that died in the upper zones and sink to the bottom. Bottom dwellers do not migrate to the upper layers that contain more food. Maybe the distance is too far, and they have little food to provide enough energy to reach it. Probably the difference in pressure is too great.[7]

BIG MOUTHS, LONG TEETH, AND FLEXIBLE STOMACHS

In the deepest zones, food is extremely limited, so animals tend to have a slow-paced lifestyle. They usually wait for food to arrive instead of spending energy hunting for it. They also spend time scavenging, which requires less energy than hunting. And when food arrives, they try to ingest as much as possible in one gulp.

Fish tend to have very large and sharp teeth, huge jaws, and names that describe them accordingly. There is the "fang tooth," the "dragon fish," the "loose jaws," and the "devil sea fish," which looks like a swimming mouth! These fish also have jaws that can be dislocated, or separated, while they gulp large chunks of food, sometimes whole animals at once.

Shaefer's anglerfish (*Sladenia shaefersi***). This is the third specimen of this species that has ever been seen.**

But what would happen if a fish swallows a very large prey? The anglerfish, for example, has an elastic stomach that can contain prey bigger than the anglerfish. Its strategy is to attract prey with a bioluminescent lure that hangs at the end of a flexible "pole" on top of its head. When prey gets close, the anglerfish snatches it whole.[8]

In spite of the lack of food, deep-sea fish tend to be larger than mesopelagic fish. Scientists think it is because deep-sea fish use most of their energy to grow. Instead, some mesopelagic fish use more energy to migrate through the water column. In general, deep-sea fish have sagging, watery muscles, weak skeletons, small eyes, and small swim bladders, if any. Deep-sea animals tend to grow slowly and live a long time. Some deep-sea clams are about one hundred years old.[9] The most common animals in the benthic zone are worms, crustaceans (crabs), clams, sea cucumbers, brittlestars, and sea stars. Two of the most impressive examples of mesopelagic marine animals are the giant and the colossal squids.

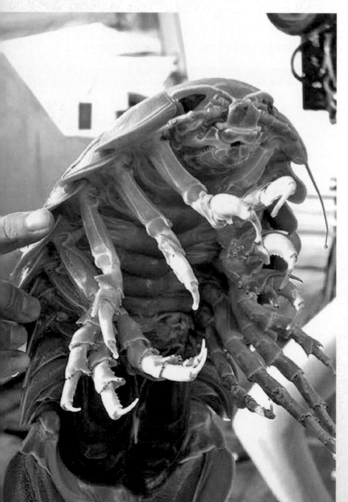

The giant deep-sea crustacean, *Bathynomis giganteus*.

THE GIANT AND THE COLOSSAL SQUIDS

The largest invertebrates on the planet are the giant and the colossal squids. They live in many oceans of the world, especially the coldest ones. The largest colossal squid found so far weighs 1,089 lbs (490 kg) while the heaviest giant squid is about 660 lbs (290 kg). However, giant squids are longer and have the longest tentacles: 18.7 feet (5.7 meters) long. They catch prey—such as 6.6-feet-long (2-meter) tooth fish—using their thorny beaks, eight arms, and two tentacles. Scientists think these squids are more the passive wait-and-catch type of hunter rather than the chase-and-catch type. Scientists from Portugal and the United States determined in 2010 that the squids have a slow-paced lifestyle, similar to other deep-sea animals. One 11-pound (5-kg) Antarctic tooth fish should suffice to provide enough food for an 1,100-pound (500-kg) colossal squid for two hundred days! Another fascinating characteristic of these squids is their eyes. They are the largest eyes in the animal kingdom—as big as soccer balls. The eyes have photophores, which they use as headlights to find prey or avoid predators, such as sperm whales, in the pitch-black, deep oceans they inhabit.[10]

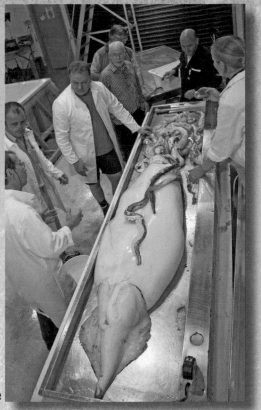

Scientists at the Museum of New Zealand Te Papa study a giant squid.

4
OASES AT THE BOTTOM OF THE SEA: HYDROTHERMAL VENTS, COLD SEEPS, AND WHALE FALLS

Some of the most amazing ecosystems on Earth lie at the very bottom of the deepest oceans.

HYDROTHERMAL VENTS

Deep down in the ocean, there are places where volcanic activity cracks open the Earth's crust. Cold seawater leaks down through the gaps and, on contact with the extremely hot magma, shoots back through the crust scalding hot (752°F or 400°C). The superheated water carries minerals from the underground rocks. The minerals precipitate, or come out of solution, when they meet the cold bottom water, looking like black smoke coming out of a chimney. The precipitates accumulate on the bottom, building chimneys—called black smokers—through which superheated water keeps venting out.

A view of the first high-temperature vent (716°F or (380°C) ever seen by scientists during a dive of the deep-sea submersible Alvin on the East Pacific Rise in 1979. This photograph shows a black smoker. Smokers can also be white, gray, or clear, depending on the material being ejected.

This is the beginning of one of the most amazing ecosystems on Earth, the hydrothermal vents.[1]

A community of living creatures not seen anywhere else grows around the vents. In contrast to all other communities studied so far, vent animals do not depend on plantlike organisms that harvest energy from sunlight through photosynthesis (light does not reach these depths). They depend on microbes that harvest energy from chemical compounds that flow out from the vents. These microbes, called chemoautotrophs, form dense mats on the outside of the chimneys, and animals eat them. There are clams, mussels, tubeworms, octopuses, fish, sea urchins, crabs, snails, sponges, worms, and sea stars. Other microbes grow inside the bodies of tube worms, clams, and mussels in a partnership that benefits both, called symbiosis. The microbes take toxic compounds, such as hydrogen sulfide (the scent of rotten eggs), and transform them into other compounds that nourish the larger animal.

Around black smokers, the superheated water emerging from the chimneys cools down significantly after mixing with the almost-freezing water that surrounds the smoker. Nevertheless, water temperature is still above what most organisms tolerate. Dr. Raymond Lee and his colleagues at Washington State University discovered that even though worms living around the smokers can tolerate 131°F (55°C)[2], they crawl toward cooler temperatures —between 104 and 122°F (40 and 50°C)—in which they can survive longer.[3]

The toughest creatures of all are microbes. The microbe that holds the record of growing at the highest temperature is rod-shaped *Methanopyrus kandleri*. It grows at 252°F (122°C)![4] The previous record holder was "Strain 121," which grows at 250°F (121°C).[5]

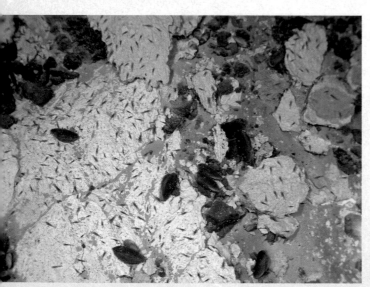

Thanks to extreme microbes, called extremophiles, more than three hundred species—95 percent of which are not found anywhere else—have found an oasis in the middle of the food-deprived bottom of the sea.[6]

Mussels and shrimp feed on white mats made of millions of bacteria around a hydrothermal vent.

COLD SEEPS

There are places at the bottom of the sea where oil and gases, such as methane and hydrogen sulfide, steadily leak out and become food for microbes. The microbes reproduce in great numbers and form thick, slimy mats that feed larger creatures. There, too, are clams, mussels, tubeworms, octopuses, fish, sea urchins, crabs, sea stars, sponges, and snails.[7] Because cold seeps are at the same temperature as the almost-freezing surrounding water, cold-seep animals grow slower and live longer than similar animals living in the vents. One cold seep tubeworm species is estimated to be more than 250 years old.[8]

A dense bed of hydrothermal mussels covers the slope of Northwest Eifuku volcano near a seafloor hot spring called Champagne vent. Other vent animals living among the mussels include shrimp, limpets, and Galatheid crabs.

WHALE FALLS

The death of a whale marks the beginning of life at the bottom of the sea. Dead whales that sink to the bottom become an abundant source of food for many bottom dwellers for decades. The first to arrive at the carcass are scavengers, such as hagfish, sleeper sharks, amphipods, and crabs. They may remove most of the skin and flesh of a thirty-ton whale in about eighteen months.

When the scavengers have finished, worms, snails, and shrimp creep up in the remains. The bone-eating zombie worms have only been found in whale carcasses. These worms extend part of their bodies into the whale's bones like plants extend roots into the ground. Microbes inside the roots break down the bone to materials the worm can feed on. Sometimes, there are so many zombie worms on a carcass that it looks like a hairy carpet.[9]

The last whale remains feed special microbes that, like those in the vents and in the cold seeps, use chemical compounds as energy sources. The microbes feeding on the

A hermit crab from a cold-seep site. Note the furry-looking covering on its claws. It is made of bacterial colonies that take toxic seep chemicals and transform them into food the crab can feed on.

A whale fall. Look closely and see that the remains of a dead whale still support a variety of marine life.

bones form thick mats that in turn feed many animals, such as mussels, clams, and worms. All together, more than thirty thousand animals have been found on a whale carcass at this point. When there is no more food, the remaining bones provide a place of safety or a support surface for animals looking for a home.

The deep seas hold the promise of new discoveries for many years to come. Will you be one of the new explorers?

HANDS-ON ACTIVITY
DIVE AND SINK

Try this experiment and see how pressure applied to an eye dropper makes it sink.

MATERIALS

- two-liter transparent soft, empty plastic bottle with cap and no label.
- water
- transparent eyedropper

PROCEDURE

1. Fill the plastic bottle to the top with water.
2. Fill the eyedropper about three-quarters with water. Leave a bubble inside.
3. Place the eyedropper inside the bottle, rubber on top.
4. Fill the bottle up to the rim and close it tightly with the cap.
5. Squeeze the middle of the bottle tightly with your hands. What happens to the dropper?
6. Stop squeezing the bottle. What happens to the dropper?

REACH YOUR CONCLUSIONS

When mammals dive deep, their lungs respond to the water pressure above them in a way similar to the bubble inside the dropper.

CHAPTER NOTES

Chapter 1. The Mysterious Deep Blue Ocean

1. Jules Verne, *20,000 Leagues Under the Sea* (New York: Signet Classic / Penguin Putnam, Inc., 2001), p. 74.

2. "Science: Diving Ball," *Time*, June 23, 1930, <http://www.time.com/time/magazine/article/0,9171,739639,00.html> (November 8, 2010).

3. "William Beebe: Going Deeper," *PBS.org*, 1999, <http://www.pbs.org/wgbh/amex/ice/sfeature/beebe.html> (November 8, 2010).

4. "Science: Low Ball," *Time*, October 3, 1932, <http://www.time.com/time/magazine/article/0,9171,744507,00.html> (November 8, 2010).

5. "Science: Deepest Down," *Time*, August 20, 1934, <http://www.time.com/time/magazine/article/0,9171,747733,00.html> (November 8, 2010).

6. Sylvia Earle, *Atlas of the Ocean: The Deep Frontier* (Washington, D.C.: National Geographic, 2001), Appendix.

7. Jennifer Hoffman, *Science 101: Ocean Science* (New York: Harper Paperbacks, 2007), p. 171.

8. Office of Satellite Data Processing and Distribution, sea surface temperature image, n.d., <http://www.osdpd.noaa.gov/data/sst/fields/FS_km5001.gif> (November 8, 2010).

9. Robert Kunzig, *The Restless Sea Exploring the World Beneath the Waves* (New York: W. W. Norton and Company, Inc., 1999), pp. 18–26.

10. "Aquarius Sea Surface Salinity From Space," *NASA*, November 3, 2010, <http://aquarius.gsfc.nasa.gov/sea_water_freeze.html> (November 8, 2010).

11. Matthias Tomczak, "Distribution of Temperature and Salinity With Depth; the Density Stratification," *Flinders University*, 2003, <http://www.es.flinders.edu.au/~mattom/IntroOc/lecture05.html> (November 9, 2010).

12. Hoffman, p. 172.

Chapter 2. Living Beneath the Sea

1. Peter Castro and Michael Huber, *Marine Biology*, 6th ed. (New York: McGraw Hill Higher Education, 2007), p. 335.

2. "Dissection of a Blue Mackerel, Scomber australasicus," *Australian Museum*, May 1998, <http://www.australianmuseum.net.au/Dissection-of-a-Blue-Mackerel-Scomber-australasicus> (November 9, 2010).

3. Terrie Williams, et al., "Sink or Swim: Strategies for Cost-efficient Diving by Marine Mammals," *Science*, vol. 288, no. 5463, April 7, 2000, pp. 133–136.

4. Peter Herring, *The Biology of the Deep Ocean* (New York: Oxford University Press, 2002), p. 110.

5. Castro and Huber, p. 362.

6. Jeffrey Graham and Kathryn Dickson, "Tuna Comparative Physiology," *Journal of Experimental Biology*, vol. 207, 2004, pp. 4015–4024.

7. Christopher B. Marshall, et al., "Hyperactive Antifreeze Proteins in a Fish," *Nature*, vol. 429, no. 6988, 2004, p. 153.

Chapter 3. Living in the Most Extreme Environments

1. Peter Herring, *The Biology of the Deep Ocean* (New York: Oxford University Press, 2002), p. 109.

2. Karen Osborn, et al., "Deep-sea, Swimming Worms With Luminescent 'Bombs,'" *Science*, vol. 325, no. 5943, August 21, 2009, p. 964.

3. Bruce Robison and Kim Reisenbichler, "Macropinna Microstoma and the Paradox of Its Tubular Eyes," *Copeia*, no. 4, 2008, pp. 780–784.

4. Alan J. Jamieson, Toyonobu Fujii, Daniel J. Mayor, Martin Solan, and Imants G. Priede, "Hadal Trenches: The Ecology of the Deepest Places on Earth," *Trends in Ecology and Evolution*, vol. 25, no. 3, March 2010, pp. 190–197.

5. Christine Dell'Amore, "New Deep-Sea Pictures: Snailfish, Eels, Found in Trench," *National Geographic News*, October 14, 2010, <http://news.nationalgeographic.com/news/2010/10/photogalleries/101014-deep-fish-seen-snailfish-eel-ocean-pictures/> (November 9, 2010).

6. Kelly Potts, "Scientists Discover New Species in One of the World's Deepest Ocean Trenches," *University of Aberdeen*, October 14, 2010, <http://www.abdn.ac.uk/news/details-9266.php> (November 9, 2010).

7. Jeffrey Levinton, *Marine Biology, Function, Biodiversity, Ecology* (New York: Oxford University Press, 2009), pp. 200–201.

8. Peter Castro and Michael Huber, *Marine Biology*, 6th ed. (New York: McGraw Hill Higher Education, 2007), pp. 365–366.

9. Ibid., p. 371.

10. "The Colossal Squid Exhibition," *Museum of New Zealand Te Papa Tongarewa*, n.d., <http://squid.tepapa.govt.nz/> (November 9, 2010).

Chapter 4. Oases at the Bottom of the Sea: Hydrothermal Vents, Cold Seeps, and Whale Falls

1. Peter Herring, *The Biology of the Deep Ocean* (New York: Oxford University Press, 2002), pp. 63–69.

2. Peter Girguis and Raymond Lee, "Thermal Preference and Tolerance of Alvinellids," *Science*, vol. 312, no. 5771, April 14, 2006, p. 231.

3. Amanda Bates, Raymond Lee, Verena Tunnicliffe, and Miles Lamare, "Deep-sea Hydrothermal Vent Animals Seek Cool Fluids in a Highly Variable Thermal Environment," *Nature Communications*, vol. 1, May 4, 2010, p. 14.

4. Ken Takai et al., "Cell Proliferation at 122°C and Isotopically Heavy CH4 Production by Hyperthermophilic Methanogen Under High Pressure Cultivation," *Proceedings of the National Academy of Sciences USA*, vol. 105, no. 31, August 5, 2008, pp. 10949–10954.

5. Kazem Kashefi and Derek R. Lovley, "Extending the Upper Temperature Limit for Life," *Science*, vol. 301, no. 5635, August 15, 2003, p. 934.

6. "Hydrothermal Vents," *National Oceanic Atmospheric Administration*, n.d., <http://www.pmel.noaa.gov/vents/nemo/explorer/concepts/hydrothermal.html> (November 9, 2010).

7. Herring, pp. 63–69.

8. Jennifer Hoffman, *Science 101: Ocean Science* (New York: Harper Paperbacks, 2007), p. 179.

9. Ibid., p. 177.

GLOSSARY

ABYSS • Something that is extremely deep.

BIOLUMINESCENCE • Light produced by living organisms.

BUOYANT • Able to float.

CHEMOAUTOTROPH • A producer organism, such as bacteria, that makes its own food using energy from chemical reactions instead of light.

CONSUMER • An organism that feeds on others.

ECTOTHERM • An animal that maintains its body temperature by absorbing heat from the environment; cold-blooded.

ENDOTHERM • An animal that maintains a constant body temperature despite changes in the environmental temperature; warm-blooded.

NEKTON • Organisms that live in water and can swim faster than currents.

PHOTOPHORE • An organ that produces bioluminescent light.

PHOTOSYNTHESIS • A process by which green plants and other organisms turn carbon dioxide and water into carbohydrates and oxygen, using light energy trapped by chlorophyll.

PLANKTON • Animals and plants that float in the ocean or swim too weakly to overcome currents.

PRODUCERS • Organisms, such as plants, that make their own food from simpler substances and a source of energy, such as light.

REFRACTION • A change in direction of a light wave when it crosses media of different densities.

SALINITY • The amount of salt or other minerals in a solution.

SCHOOLMATE • A companion in a school of fish.

SEA SNOW • Small particles that fall to the bottom of the ocean made of the remains of dead aquatic creatures.

FURTHER READING

Books

Collard III, Sneed B. *In the Deep Sea.* Tarrytown, N.Y.: Marshall Cavendish Benchmark, 2006.

Newquist, H. P. *Here There Be Monsters: The Legendary Kraken and the Giant Squid.* Boston, Mass.: Houghton Mifflin Children's Books, 2010.

Nouvian, Claire. *The Deep: The Extraordinary Creatures of the Abyss.* Chicago: University of Chicago Press, 2007.

Sheldon, David. *Into the Deep: The Life of Naturalist and Explorer William Beebe.* Watertown, Mass.: Charlesbridge, 2009.

Internet Addresses

The Colossal Squid Exhibition
<http://squid.tepapa.govt.nz/>

Leatherback Turtle
<http://www.nmfs.noaa.gov/pr/species/turtles/leatherback.htm>

MarineBio.org: The Deep Sea
<http://marinebio.org/oceans/deep/index.asp>

Ana María Rodríguez's Web site
<http://www.anamariarodriguez.com>

INDEX